To,

My Grandparents. I know you would have been proud.
Mr. Jayant Mankame. I wish I had some more time with you.
Everyone on the Road to Recovery. Stay Strong. This is for you.

My sincere and heartfelt thanks to-

The one who taught me to lose myself in poetry,
Marshall Mathers a.k.a. Eminem, The Real Slim Shady.

Vandana and Chandrashekhar Nilvarna, my mother and
father,
For sacrificing and working for me harder.

Santosh Breed, my role model and my entire family,
For keeping me happy.

A best friend and a brother,
Aditya Rasam, for taking my mind further.

Shreya Shahane, Durva Naik and Gargi Ranade,
For being my editors and teaching me along the way.

Adesh Purandare, Nishant Gaonkar,
For being great friends and brothers.
Tanvi Sanghavi and Surbhi Dhoot,
For motivation and keeping skies blue.
Emma Monschein, Emily Poitras, Bella Alcock, Tash, Khushi
Kumar, Beto Tox, Ilja Kim,
For helping me to keep smiling.

Everyone who gave me the hard times,
You enhanced my thought and created the rhymes.

Patridge publications for their endless support.

Preface

Dear you,

A reminder that you are an amazing person. You have a beautiful smile. You are a powerful person who can make a change. You have an inner strength in you. You are a superhero in your own unique way. So take a deep breath. Fill yourself with the energy around you. Smile for yourself. Close your eyes and say "I am amazing"

That's what matters. You matter. You make a difference. Without you the world would be incomplete. You are worth something which cannot be valued. You are perfect. You have overcome every bad thing in your life. Be proud of that. Your worst days have been fought hard by you! You are strong! You are a perfect combination of beautiful imperfections.

Be unique. Be yourself. Spread love!

Contents

Birth

Isn't it so beautiful?
Watching someone for the first time in this world,
A mother is born along with the child,
After going through so much of torment,
A world full of mysteries,
A new mind is developed,
A new soul is shaped,
A new way of thinking comes into existence,
The world will shape you,
Or you can shape the world.

Family

As I see you smile,
The words stop flowing,
The mind travels a thousand miles,
The darkness starts glowing,
7 billion people around,
Isn't it so wonderful,
That still, you are the one I have found,
The one who makes every moment cheerful,
What they say is correct,
Soulmates are found and not searched,
Your imperfections together are perfect,
Their resonance is your world,
Highly complicated this life,
One step wrong you end up below,
It's a very sharp pointed knife,
Whose slightest cut makes your blood flow,
In this vast universe,
You are the one who sets me free,
Makes me live before reaching the hearse,
You are the roots to my tree,
Now I know for sure,
Your light will end my nights,
Your smile will be my cure,
Your hope will take me to heights,
You don't make me want to change myself,
Making me love who I am,
You need to know something about yourself,
You are my soulmate, friend and who I am.

Memories

One day,
I was just lost in my thoughts,
A place of endless feelings,
A place where it's unsafe for everyone else,
As I enter the place,
I stand in the middle,
Suddenly a flashback starts,
The lights go out,
A cinematic scenario starts,
The film plays,
I see all the old memories,
The good ones, the bad ones,
Slowly the good ones fade away,
The bad memories get brighter,
They are all around me,
I smile and try to make them go away,
But nothing works.
I see the times I made mistakes,
The times I screwed up,
The times I let myself down,
I feel trapped,
Everything around me crumbles,
It's all just a barren land now,
I stand there alone,
The place feels so empty,
Suddenly somebody comes to me,
That somebody grabs my hand,
Smiles at me,
That somebody gives me strength which I've never experienced
before,

Suddenly flowers and grass start growing around,
I see a beautiful butterfly,
The sun rises,
The good memories come back,
That's what one person can make a difference,
All that somebody did was stand by my side,
The somebody never gave up and always smiled,
Because of that somebody,
I am so happy,
I am so positive,
I feel so amazing,
That somebody is you

The First Realizations

Don't worry about the weather,
The wetter the better,
This will nurture you,
Like a small seed in you.

You need rough time,
To cherish your existence,
But don't always be in bad time,
Grab happiness at once.

You are a daisy in a field of roses,
Different amidst others,
But I'd always choose a daisy,
Because rose becomes so cheesy.

You need to realise,
What others say doesn't define you,
You are something much more,
Something much better than the morning dew.

You need not know yourself,
Or maybe describe it to others,
Just feel things,
Words can't suffice every feelings.

Hey Little Fighter

Hey little fighter,
Things will get brighter,
Don't you give up yet,
Days ahead will be the best.
You have to believe in yourself,
If you feel trapped just shout Help,
I'll be there to listen,
Your happiness is my Mission.
The things look dark,
But you have a spark,
The stars will guide you,
Towards a happiness true.
Some things will take time,
But you have to wait for a while,
Cause even if you stay sad for long,
Your happiness ahead will sing a different song.
Just remember my little fighter,
The things will get better

Fate

Why should the lines on your palm,
Decide your fate?
Your soul is such a beautiful house,
Why to enclose it inside doors of hate?

You are a firefly,
Waiting to create it's own destiny,
Waiting for the night to light it up,
Like a day so sunny.

You write your own destiny,
Take the words and lines,
Write them on a rampage,
Such that your success shines.

Learning

You are responsible,
For making me the person I am,
For motivating me,
For helping me to develop,
No words can express,
How thankful I am,
To have a teacher like you,
In my life.
Like a mother,
You held my hand,
Took me on this wonderful journey,
Where I learned,
Where I developed myself.
I'll have to agree,
That you are no less than a mother.
Thank you so much.
Teachers are rightfully next to God,
Everyone is a teacher,
Everyone is a student.

Poverty

Hello there,
Please don't ignore me,
Please give me something,
I am hungry.

You will go about with your day,
Someone will smile on seeing you,
I will go about asking others,
I wish I could be you,

But I am not complaining,
And I surely won't be chasing you,
But please see me at the side of the road,
I am not begging you to.

My cousins are dying,
Oh they don't live here Sir,
They live in the hot sands across the sea,
I was told by the flying bird.

I don't like begging like this,
I am not poor by choice,
Yes some false people have eroded your faith,
But they are well trained boys.

I am thirsty Mam,
I am not the only child,
We all are waiting to be fed,
By a mother who hasn't returned for a while.

When you play at the waterparks,
We search for a drop to drink,
When you have the big meals,
We wait in the corner to get something to eat.

Oh no Sir,
I am not asking you to pity us,
Or we don't want you to stop,
But why would you think of nobody like us?

I will sleep in the beautiful cloth,
The cloth of my bare skin,
You will sleep in your big homes,
In beds of silk and satin.

Some of us are all by our own,
Waiting for someone to come,
The wait never ends Sir,
We all Fall down eventually.

A terrorist attack gets so much love,
Oh we do mourn the lives lost,
But we are terrorised too!
By guns of greed and bullets of promises false.

No one comes to feed our babies,
No one thinks of making us smile,
My Brothers die of diseases daily,
Oh please tell me why?

Is it our fault that we are born here?
Tell me what have you done to be born there?
Oh I am not complaining Sir,
I just wish to live there.

I am sorry to take up your precious time,
But if you get a Chance to See,
Turn away for some time,
You will find me trying to breathe.

I know I will die soon,
Please let others live for a while,
No I am not sad Sir,
It doesn't take money or food to share a smile.

A Revenge

I am cold as the cold Wind blows,
Crushing dreams and killing hopes.

A sunny day in the town,
People with smiles, he was with a frown.
"Hey you little fella!"
"Get off my lawn with your brother."
The Kid started crying,
His brother did stop moving,
An object flew out of the window,
The house itself seemed impressed with the throw.
The boys ran away,
The frown turned to a smile that day.
Mr. Crossfire went inside,
His house was the best to hide.
The boys left the town next month,
To treat their eldest son.
Now I am in his cupboard,
His footsteps can be heard,
I feel so high looking through the gaps,
A Rat after a 100 traps.

As the storm rages on,
Mr. Crossfire puts the heater on,
I come out with a smile,
Throw the object with the style,
His expression was worth it,
On the other side came a man trying,
To handle his gun aiming at me,
We both let our arms set free,
Only 1 Person died,
Yeah we tried,
Oh he died in the Cross Fire,
Goodbye,
We don't expect anything further,
Let's go brother.

A Bond Broken Before Time

He lay there with his eyes closed,
The smell of Hospital,
The machine beeped his existence,
During his last few hours.

The smile wore off,
Looking into his eyes,
Knowing that it would be for the last time,
Heaven wanted him in the skies.

Holding my Hand firmly,
He managed a feeble smile,
"Don't cry and just smile"
The voice was heard for one last time.

The waves became flat,
The Hand became cold,
I wish I could tell him,
We were supposed to die together old.

You Are Not Alone

Lost in the world so grey,
Looking for someone you can call home,
Someone who'll care and stay,
Someone you can call your own.

Don't you worry now,
I got your back,
You may wonder how,
Close distance is what we lack.

Beautiful things happen over a distance,
You just have to realise that,
I'm everything you need at once,
A friend, a listener or even a hat!

You are not alone my friend,
There are many who feel the same,
Many who feel lost seeing just the end,
Thinking about quitting the game.

You are not alone my friend,
Not in your feelings or even reality,
Your heart is what we can mend,
You'll shine in the middle of the city.

This World

A new morning,
Can it be a new beginning?
Why is the world this way?
Oh I don't know why I am,
Trying to understand the world,

On the pressure of Fame,
On the influence of wealth,
Resides the world.

Fangs of Terror,
Poison of fear,
It is a Snake, this world.

Burning other's lives,
Burning other's settlements,
Settles this world.

Killing the smiles on the faces,
Stopping everyone's laughter,
Laughs this world.

Teaches us meanings,
Dominates with Power,
How clever is this world.

I think,
It is capable of surviving it'self,
This world.

Why only humans?
Even Jesus was killed,
By This world.

Am I not a human?
Losing myself in the void,
My soul floats in the thoughts of this world,
I try to please everyone,
But there stays no one,
I look up to the skies,
I just wanted to make everyone happy,
Why does my looks have to matter?
When my thoughts could travel?

I take the gun in my Hand,
I was just about to pull the Trigger,
When there came a figure,
It asked me to stop.
The world is what you want it to be,
It can trap you or set you free.

A child's cry,
A mother's love,
A father's care is this world.

A smile with a tear,
A happy laughter,
A day with no fear is this world.

The world is yours,
Doesn't matter if you,
Are a boy or a girl too.
I put aside the gun,
Just then Rose the sun,
A new Beginning,
A new Hope,
That maybe someday,
They will accept me for who I am,
And my thoughts,
Would see the light of the day.

Losing Myself

Lately it seems as if it is,
Me against the world,
Every try is a miss,
Expecting every stone to be emerald,
Assuming I have people,
To look up to when I'm not even,
The chances of being odd are feeble,
In the alligator pit like Irwin Steven,
Day in, day out,
Sometimes loudly, sometimes silently,
I cry, I shout,
Till the horizon is visible hazily.

A Simple Feeling

Let me tell you a story of a girl,
Whose eyes were brighter than the pearl.

She was always alone,
No one would text or call her on her phone.

She wanted to die,
Move towards the heaven in sky.

She started to cut herself,
She hid the blades in her shelf.

She was always bullied,
She was tired and wanted to scream.

She tried to get away,
But everyone made her stay.

Then came a guy,
Who also used to cry,

He knew what was to be sad,
He was getting really mad,.

They both talked,
Till both of them had cried.

They got a feeling of happiness,
And a relief from stress.

They became best friends too,
Trusted each other so true.

I don't know the ending of this story,
I hope we find out together

The Rains

Here comes the rain,
Reminding me of the rivers of sorrows,
Of the birds that never flew.

Connecting all the dots of pain,
I look ahead for a better tomorrow,
But all I want to feel is the wind that never flew.

A fast feeling of emptiness,
Collecting inside my heart,
Why did you do this to me?

You created a beautiful mess,
But you did tear it apart,
I wandered alone in the sea.

It's 12 in the night,
I should be asleep,
Instead I'm wide awake, wondering.

Was I wrong or were they right?
Why did they cause a wound so deep?
Trapped by a thorny ring.

The more I try to suppress the thoughts,
Of you and everyone who didn't care,
I sleep a little less and I cry a little more.

I've trusted you with secrets of all sorts,
Now at 1am into the darkness I stare,
Looking at the wall, lying on the floor.

I'm reminded of all my pain,
The hope of getting better tomorrows,
The tree of loneliness grew.

Here comes the rain,
Reminding of the rivers of sorrows,
Of the birds that never flew.

The Tough Times Shall Pass

Your life seems so complicated,
You don't see any way out of it,
Everything's spinning in your head,
It seems like an endless pit.
But don't you give up,
This bad time shall pass,
Just breathe and look up,
And absorb the strength from the stars.
You will keep fighting,
However long it takes,
You will learn to sing,
In the world so fake.
You feel you are changed,
You aren't the person you were,
The old you is dead,
Because people change only for the better.
The sun will shine again,
In the sea of your life,
To remove all your pain,
Choose a flower and not a knife.
I am not a fortune teller,
I can't predict the future,
But I'm sure it's better,
Because you are stronger than you were.
You can do it,
I believe in you,
You can make through it,
I believe in you.

Beautiful

The way she smiled at the sun,
Looks like she's having fun,
I saw her at the previous turn,
Look how beautiful she is.

The smile on her pretty face,
The freckles say hello there,
And her curly hair,
Look how beautiful she is.

Then I reach up close to her,
My mind went up for a stir,
The most perfect girl,
Look how beautiful she is.

I saw her hands with scars,
Her life would have been so damn harsh,
I called her from afar,
Look how beautiful she is.

She looked at me and she smiled,
But I knew eyes had lied,
And the life has died,
Still how beautiful she is.

She told me how she can't be,
The perfect girl for him,
And for no one in the society,
Look how beautiful she is.

With the scars still on her wrists,
The pain still in her heart,
She decided to let it go and start again,
Look how beautiful she is.

With the new strength,
And new hope,
I see her smile truly,
Look how she beautiful she is.

Who says girls with scars aren't beautiful?
Who says girls suicidal aren't beautiful?
Who says depressed ones aren't beautiful?

You Are Going To Shine So Bright

7 billion people in the world,
You might see yourself,
As just someone in this herd,
Just another book in a library shelf.
But, every book has a reader,
You are not alone,
You'll find your reader,
You'll find someone you call home.
Even if the times seem hard sometimes,
The sun doesn't seem to shine,
But your heart still sings the rhymes,
With a feeling in each line.
You just keep matching the notes,
Keep dancing with yourself,
Even if in the sea you don't see the boats,
Go on swimming to find yourself.
Soon you'll reach where you want to go,
It might take a little long,
Don't ever let your patience go,
Time is what makes the Diamond strong.
When you'll be dancing in the dark,
You are going to light up the night,
Like a shooting star,
You are going to shine so bright.

The Past

Sometimes a ghost haunts you,
The ghost you've known,
It makes you cry too,
It has grown.

It's the ghost of past,
It can be dangerous,
But don't worry, it won't last,
It'll be afraid of us.

Let's make a beautiful present,
The past is past,
Let's make it end,
The future may come slow or fast.

It's uncertain what your life will be,
I'm no fortune teller,
But I'll make it a cherry blossom tree,
And. make you smile brighter.

Just kick the ghost of past,
Stop them tears,
Let's make that sadness the last,
And overcome the fears

You Are Special

Even if I searched,
The deep seas,
The high mountains,
The dense forests,
The dry deserts,
Even if the world turns upside down,
Or it does get destroyed,
Even if we contact aliens,
Or if animals could speak,
Even if I could revive the dead,
Or give life to fictional characters,
Never would I find,
Someone so caring,
Someone so crazy,
Someone so beautiful,
But someone so lazy,
Someone who'd give up everything,
Someone who'd fight the world,
Someone who has a beautiful heart,
There is no 2nd,
There will never ever be,
Someone like you

You Are Beautiful

The stars seem to shine upon you,
The moon tries to hide,
The flowers are jealous of you,
You are a beach on a high tide.
You are so beautiful!

You may not love yourself,
Or maybe even hate,
But just once see yourself,
Through my eyes' gate,
You are so beautiful!

The smile, the eyes,
The beautiful face and beautiful hair,
Reflecting the earth and the skies,
I could just forever stare,
You are so beautiful!

Don't let anyone tell you,
You ain't beautiful,
Because they don't see the real you,
And they just make themselves a fool,
You are so beautiful!

No weight is over,
No face is prettier,
No one's beauty is higher or lower,
Everyone is beautiful and unique here,
You are so beautiful!

Just keep smiling always,
Don't lose that smile,
Because that's what completes your face,
That's who you are and that's your style,
You are so beautiful!

Smile

Even when you find no reason,
JUST SMILE.

Think about a little child playing,
Think about your best friend waving,
Think about the thing,
That makes you smile.
Think about an old couple sitting,
Laughing together with the sun rising,
Think about the day you had fun,
You were yourself and you felt the sun.
Think about your favourite celebrity,
You and they having a cup of tea.
Think about everything that makes you smile,
Make your day happy and worthwhile.
Even if you find nothing,
Don't even worry about anything,
Just force yourself to a smile,
That's your fashion, that's your style!
Just smile without a reason immediately,
I want your time to go beautifully!

Even when you find no reason,
JUST SMILE!!

A Phoenix In You

Why do we fall?
So that we can learn to get back up,
But to get back up,
You need to have a belief.
A belief that you are something,
You are stronger than you think,
You can rise higher than you think,
But you stop yourself.
You fear the society,
You have your name written on a throne,
Which is made of gold and not stone,
You just need to have belief.
The cave you are in,
Is long, dark and filled with bugs,
You'll also find the haters and the thugs,
It won't be easy.
But it isn't impossible too,
Get a torch light,
Get into the night,
You have to just believe in yourself.
Keep moving ahead,
Even if the torch dies,
Let the spark in you guide,
Follow the light at the end of the tunnel.
Seize every small opportunity,
You are capable of things you don't know,
You are a seed which is yet to grow,
Just take a deep breath and rise.

Failures lead the way to success,
So don't you give up yet,
You haven't reached till your best,
Wake the phoenix in your heart.
There are ashes from the past,
The phoenix will rise again,
You'll rise by burning your pain,
It is up to you to stay down or rise high.

Feel Proud

If no one told you this today,
I know how much difficult it is,
To be strong in this world so grey,
But you have been through this.
You have survived so much,
You should be proud.

I feel so happy now,
Looking at how far you have come,
I still wonder how,
How can you be so strong?
You have survived so much.
You should be proud.

Now don't you give up yet,
You've come so far,
Don't be tired yet,
You have been strong so far.
You have survived so much.
You should be proud.

The storm will end soon,
There will be a rainbow,
Your name will be with the moon,
Your happiness will grow.
You have survived so much.
You should be proud.

Your smile is worth a million,
So smile big!
You have survived so much,
You should be proud!
I am proud of you!

Being Selfless

Think of yourself first,
But is it necessarily so?
Do we really deserve it?
One day we came and soon we'll go.
What do we make of our lives?
We rush, we try, we pray,
My house, my City, my State,
Aiming at being happy each day.

A child asked his father,
"Dad what is a happy life?"
His dad smiled and said,
It is living and not being just alive,
The story didn't end here,
The next day the son returned,
A troubled face in the small house,
"Dad what is happy life?"
Drowsy and tired due to work,
"Son! I told you yesterday!"
"I know, but is it a happy life,
When you can't make others happy?"

Isn't it so fascinating?
We all want to be happy and at peace,
But we can't make others happy,
To be or not to be was the question,
Even after just being,

To be for yourself or for others,
Why isn't that the question?
We are mere symbols of existence,
We are not responsible for it,
Like the great minds think.

Being selfless isn't so difficult,
Just a small effort does a lot.
Before you know,
A child has survived a drought,
A girl is learning Alphabet,
A teen hasn't jumped off the edge,
An old man has smiled after long,
The birds have found their song,
Mother nature is smiling,

The day you live for others,
The day you forget the wrongs,
That is the day when,
Moksha comes rushing in.
Moksha isn't liberalisation,
It is the defining Moment of your mind.
Your heart has desires,
Your mind has the power to achieve them.
The main Strength is your mind.

We do need an Apocalypse,
Apocalypse of our inner selves,
A new Beginning,
A new Desire of being,
Being selfless.

You Can Win This

Even if you seem to be losing,
And you have lost your soldiers,
Just don't stop fighting,
This can get a bit worse.

We'll pick up the worst,
Make it the best,
Even if your life seems cursed,
We will get through this test.

Every storm ends with a rainbow,
Every caterpillar turns to butterfly,
You life will go to extreme low,
But it'll reach to sky high.

So get your strength together,
Throw them tears in the bin,
I will fight with you forever,
This is a fight you can win!

A Fallen Warrior

What do we do when we fall down?
What do we do when we are kicked down?
When everyone pushes you down?
Makes your self esteem very low?
When you don't believe in yourself?
When that happens,
We need to just do 1 thing,
Fight till our strength sharpens,
If they are loud, just sing,
Haters going to hate,
But you don't have to give up,
Cause it's just not your fate,
To never get back up!
It may take a day, a week or a year,
Just gather your strength,
And keep moving ahead without a fear,
Get back up with your pride,
Just face the challenge and pain,
Don't even try to hide,
The struggle is bad,
But never give up,
And one day you'll get back up,
Just like a fallen warrior!

A Wallflower

As the sun rises and sets again,
Things look bleak and you feel pain,
The feelings cannot be endured,
You feel like you are being murdered.
But look in the mirror,
Look at the emotions that stir,
You are not weak,
Not even a bit sick.
You are not different,
Don't be so reluctant,
You need to believe in yourself,
Throw the blade off the shelf.
Remove the demons from your mind,
Think of the days when the sun shined,
There was no rain upon you
Just happiness pure and true.
You need to let the sadness go,
Because it has to be so,
Believe in yourself and stay strong,
Depression isn't any thing wrong,
Don't jump off the tower,
Because you are a beautiful wallflower!

Broken Arrows

Sometimes you are losing,
But sometimes you are shooting,
Broken arrows in the dark,
But I see the hope in your heart.

Your arms deserve flowers and petals,
Not the shiny blades or cutters,
The shine should be on your face,
And not on the silver blade.

You may be losing the battle,
But you are the one who matters,
The leaves are falling,
But spring is coming.

The water from the river is drying,
You can't stop yourself from crying,
But the fishes who need the water,
For them you matter.

The billion cells in your body,
Working together for you, a beauty,
You are a garden,
Made of flowers a million.

Rise above everything,
Be a Phoenix rising,
Come back from the ashes,
Leave everyone else in shushes.

Sometimes you are losing,
But sometimes you are shooting,
Broken arrows in the dark,
But I see the hope in your heart.

A New Start

Whatever has happened has happened,
Whatever was meant to be has been,
You can't change the past now,
You can't change what you have seen.

So take a moment to choose,
What deserves to go ahead,
Is it the tears cried,
Or the joys ahead?

Leave the bad memories,
And the poor decisions,
Take the proud moments,
And your mighty visions.

What matters is what you take with you,
To the year so fresh and new,
Let's make a beautiful year,
Which is all about you.

So keep the joys and keep the smiles,
Leave the sadness aside,
This is a new start,
With a smile very wide.

First Love

What is this feeling?
I feel numb when I'm with you,
I feel the whole world at my feet,
Even bright yellow feels blue.
That smile,
Those dimples on your cheeks,
It's going to take a while to realise,
Weeks, months or even years.
What is this feeling?
I can see you everywhere,
Maybe I'm just dreaming,
But why do I get the scent of your hair?
In a room full of people,
Why is the spotlight on you?
The warmth will burn the haystack and the needle,
My mind and heart have no clue.
What is this feeling?
I don't know if it is love,
I don't know what it is,
But all I know is that this is beautiful,
But if you know please tell me,
What is this feeling?

If Tomorrow Is The Last Day

If tomorrow is the last day,
There won't be any day after,
Will you be with me today?
Spend the time with laughter?
If the skies fall,
I'll never let go.

If there was a chance,
Of any one of us to live,
I'll just give you a last glance,
And jump on the side so deep,
If the skies fall,
I'll never let go.

If times go hard,
If maybe the sun doesn't shine anymore,
I'll carve out my heart,
Burn it to give you heat and let you live more,
If the skies fall,
I'll never let go.

If tomorrow is the happiest day,
If it is going to change my world,
Would you smile and stay?
Would you celebrate like a bird?
If the skies fall,
I'll never let go.

If we live and cherish the moments,
If we just smile and forget the ends,
Would you smile all the way,
Would you enjoy every day?
Because I promise,
If the skies fall,
I'll never let go.

This Love

So many happy smiles,
A few tears together,
We've come forward a 1000 miles,
We are here no matter what the weather.
I see the world when I see your face,
The fireworks in the sky,
Like a tiger's rage,
I've felt my tears easily dry.
I promise I'll always be here,
But even if something happens,
You keep me always dear,
Even if your problems weigh tons,
Even if our distance increases to infinity,
My heart will still be with you,
Like the centre of a city,
My love for you is so very true.
I know I get so sentimental and so stupid,
But this is something you should know,
Memories should never get buried,
And your smile is all that I want to glow.
So carry on my best friend,
You are very special,
My love for you will never end,
And you for me are celestial.
You hold my heart so feeble,
But you all are that I have.

A Setback

I stay awake in the middle of the night,
Wondering where you are,

I don't know what I feel,
This is what undefined feels like,
But life is beautiful,
But is it all that it's like?

I feel hurt at times when you don't speak,
But this is what this journey is I guess,
You are nice to everyone,
I love your kindness.

Our goodnights repeat so many times,
Haha I so don't want to let you go,
Just keep talking,
Something more and more.

I love when you get all serious,
You seem so mature,
Maybe I will keep believing in everything you say,
You have a heart so pure.

The jealousy thing was raw,
I regret saying it,
But that's the truth I guess,
Never going to give in.

I feel sad now,
I don't know why,
I feel like living,
But I do want to die.

I love you so much,
You make me smile,
Maybe you would never love me,
Not now, not in a while.

I wish you could see,
How much I love you,
But you have your beautiful life,
Why would you want sadness so true!

All I wish is that you stay happy,
Never be sad, or never ever cry,
I am stupid and crazy,
But I want to get better and I try!

I expected someone to understand me,
Everyone left one by one,
In the end I would end up,
Sitting somewhere crying beneath the sun.

The Darkest Moments

The blank times,
When nothing is visible,
The sky is dark, the moon is dark,
And nothing is feasible.
To the starry nights,
That no one seems to see,
But when you have darkness,
That's all I wish to see.
I'm scared to venture in the dark,
But I don't want to just wait either,
All I wish to see is a tiny spark,
And get a breather.
But the walls keep closing in,
You don't see a way out,
These are the times when you see,
That you have to find a way out.
The darkness engulfs,
But you see a light,
It's getting swallowed by the darkness,
But you give it a fight.
In the rush of things,
You get through the dark,
You reach the light,
And find that you had created the spark.
You rescued yourself,
With a spark from within,
It was just highlighted,
By mirrors of hope,
And the darkness got eradicated.

Dreams

Dreams take you higher,
Dreams give you hope,
To stop you from falling,
Dreams are the rope.

You need to dream,
About a better you,
To become a happy person,
To make the sky blue.

Dreams make you smile,
Dreams keep you going,
Even if your life is sad,
Dreams make it mind blowing.

Dreams won't make it better,
Or they won't be super magical,
But dreams give you a direction,
And say that change is possible.

Dreams take you to a different zone,
Where you can win,
So whenever you feel lost,
Close your eyes and dream

The times can be bad,
Your insides are screaming,
Things will get better,
Just Never stop dreaming!

The Real Treasure

All of the skies speak to me,
That the new day will dawn,
The forests will echo with laughter,
I'll find the stairway to heaven.

But I'll not be alone,
They say there'll be someone,
A bird willing to fly,
And sing along and hum,

Together we'll move along,
Towards the end of the road,
And not stop there,
But move towards the heaven above.

Crossing the lakes,
Swimming across,
Tall mountains lie ahead,
The fear goes for a toss.

There's a feeling I get,
When I look at you,
My spirit goes for a spin,
The grey skies turn blue.

The adventure is tough,
The journey is too long,
But the companion I have,
Cannot let me go wrong.

You make me wonder,
The real riches are true,
They are not gold or money,
It is no one but you.

One Day At A Time

If the problems seem to mount,
Make sure you don't panic out.
The best is yet to come,
So make sure you don't run.
Things can get real bad,
Stuck to the sea bed.
Where you can't get going,
And you are drowning.
Remember, all the big stories,
And the famous histories,
Are not made in a single day,
You have to find a way,
You have to be patient,
Things will build up,
You'll find your way to paradise,
A happy and peaceful life,
The problems will fade away,
Night will turn to day,
New sun will rise,
Darkness will see it's demise,
Just keep a thing in mind,
Remember to always smile,
And take it one day at a time.

Breathe In, Breathe Out

Breathe in, breathe out,
Feel any different?
I think you don't, no one does,
Breathing the air like everyone.

Now open up your book,
Tear a page, and throw it away,
Keep doing this and buy new ones,
Just for 1 day.

You won't feel any different,
No one would,
But to satisfy your need,
We would lose 100 sources of wood.

We grow so fast,
Regardless of the things around,
But without even realising,
The trees die without making a sound.

We call forests our lungs,
But we trade them ourselves,
Burning, destroying them,
For increasing the size of our shelves.

Start from today,
Vow to avoid wastage,
The lungs are dying too fast,
We need to extend their age.

Avoid using paper wherever possible,
Every small effort will count,
Plant a tree every chance you get,
Let's make things better around.

Soon, a day will come,
However loud we may shout,
It will be impossible,
To just Breathe in, breathe out.

Make Memories

Isn't it so fascinating to wonder,
That some years ahead,
Your future self will sit,
To cherish the memories in your head,
The memories which will be created,
By you today,
The person you are now,
Will be remembered by you right away.
In some future time,
He's watching you smile,
Watching you learn and grow,
All in his mind.
Memories are beautiful,
But choose which ones to Keep,
We want us to smile always,
So delete the ones where you weep.
But be careful my dear friend,
Some weeping memories,
Are the ones which made you change,
They all have some certain stories.
These stories will make your future,
So live them to the most,
You'll need some warm memories,
When you get covered with frost.

Keep Moving Ahead

Never quit,
Just keep on going,
If you can't run, then walk,
If you can't walk, keep crawling!
Every success comes with failure,
With a feeling to give up,
To just shut off everything,
And drench in the rain drop,
But don't you dare to quit now,
Every success makes you fall,
But by getting over them,
You'll get joy so tall,
If your wing is injured,
Or if your beak is a little bent,
Never stop to keep flying,
Don't let your journey end,
It's not so easy,
But it isn't impossible,
Be a warrior strong,
And no effort is too little,
You are amazing,
Destined to be great,
Just fall seven times,
But stand up eight!

Towards The Greater World

Stepping on the backs,
Of these poor eyes,
What makes us say we are humans,
If we kill in broad daylight?
A 1000 billion spent in war,
But just a 100 could have sufficed,
To end the biggest war,
Of the poor and their poverty.
We become the fishes,
Make everything available in a market,
In a market under the sea,
But these birds can't even get past the gate.
Some say it's their destiny,
Or it's because they are criminals,
Haven't we ever committed a crime?
Why aren't we all equals?
The biggest criminals aren't those,
Who steal to fill their stomach,
They are those who keep eating,
Even after eating too much.
We all are humans,
We all deserve to live,
So why does a baby die,
While the other learns to fly?

It's just so disproportionate,
How the poor get poor,
And the rich get richer,
It needs to change for sure.
The small hungry eyes,
Look at you with hope,
Luxury is a good elevator,
But they have survival as their rope.
So be a human my friend,
We all can do a thing or two,
Donate, help, volunteer,
Let's make the world happy and blue.

A Little Something For You

Hey you,
I've got something to tell you,
A tiny little secret,
You'll love it I bet,
You are wonderful,
A one in a billion,
No one can ever be you,
No matter what they ever do,
You don't need someone else,
To show you what you can be,
You just have to keep faith in yourself,
Be the best book on the shelf,
Life is something you regret,
Maybe you need some love,
But you have to keep in mind,
Love isn't so hard to find,
Love for yourself should,
Come from inside you and within,
Not from anyone outside,
To help your sorrows to hide,
You will help you grow,
And maybe you will love you the most,
But for that, first love yourself,
And you will develop yourself,
What you expect from others,
Try to get it from within,
Love yourself more than what you expect from others,
Make yourself smile and wipe the tears.

A Letter From A Bird

Do you hear me?
Oh does anyone hear me?
My insides are hurting,
My throat is burning,
I can't see anything,
My friend has lost her voice to sing,
All we see is distant smoke,
You know how my leg broke?
I was sitting on a huge structure,
When a person like you hurt,
You laughed when I cried,
You ignored when my brother died,
Oh I'm so hungry now,
I'll eat with my friend, the cow,
What is that shiny thing?
Is that a long shiny string?
Ow, it's so hard to eat,
Let me try and swallow fully,
It's not so tasty,
But it filled my stomach totally,
Oh it's hurting again!
I need water, make it rain!
There's no water around,
Some black fluid is what I found,
Where are the blue lakes?
Why are there just shipwrecks?
Where are the green lush forests?
Why the artificial structures for our nests?

My father told me,
He could fly to a hundred trees,
Eat fresh fish and fruits,
Drink fresh water too,
I want to live more,
Ow my stomach is going to burst open!
My throat is burning,
The black fluid is choking!
Flying around trying to see,
Please set me free!
Would you still care the same?
If your child had to suffer the same?

Does anyone hear me?

Imagine

Imagine.
Imagine a world so happy,
With no place for sadness,
With no one to cry,
With everything selfless.

Imagine a day so beautiful,
With the sun shining so bright,
With the clouds dancing around,
With the birds never out of sight.

Imagine a nature,
Where trees stand instead of concrete,
Where birds and animals don't die,
Where we both share the same street.

Imagine the hearts so pure,
With only care for everyone,
With no envy, hatred or evilness,
With a space for flower and not a gun.

Imagine the society so just,
With no discrimination,
With no inequality,
With only love and affection.

Imagine the countries together,
With no borders between,
With a single big world,
With everyone achieving their dream.

Imagine yourself at your best,
With no sadness or regrets,
With just happiness and smiles,
With a thousand friends.

It is easy to imagine,
It'll be easy to achieve,
Only we have to be together,
And change the way we perceive.

Just imagine everything perfect,
With no negativity,
Everyone together happy,
Only filled with positivity.

The Bright Light

No moment lasts forever,
This shall pass too,
Your mind will take leaps ahead,
The rain will stop, sky will be blue.
The darkness will disappear,
Your happiness will light up the world,
You just have to hold on,
Just make sure you are heard.
Heard by someone who'll stay,
Through the darkness,
Hold your hand and lead the way,
Out of this crazy mess.
You are a bird destined to fly,
Don't let anyone tell you different,
Your bad times will pass away,
Your eyes will sparkle like diamonds.
So just hold on and drive patiently,
Keep your headlights on through the night,
Soon around the corner,
You'll find the bright light

Depression

I come as I go,
No one needs to know,
I grow some flowers on myself,
Where bees sit along,
Soon when I need water,
And the thirst takes over,
The bees sting everywhere.
Like the legend of Rome,
I wasn't built in a day,
The longer you stare at me,
The more you start to hate.
I am everywhere around you,
But I can be nowhere if I want.

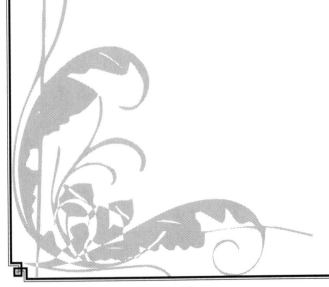

Towards The Sun

When you feel no hope,
when you feel no strength,
Let go of the fears around you,
Turn your face towards the sun,
Let the shadow fall behind you!

A flower so small,
Unable to grow,
You are caught up in a dream,
Into the waters, trying to row.

Don't look at the side that you won't,
Look at the side where you will,
The Wind blows towards you,
To move your boat which is still.

Look at the brighter side,
A sky so blue, a day so bright,
Close your eyes and smile inside,
Away from the dark night.

When you feel no hope,
When you feel no strength,
Let go of the fears around you,
Turn your face towards the sun,
Let the shadow fall behind you!

Celestial

Beneath the stars I sit,
Is it the Wind or is it the sky?
The mind plays a game of emotions,
The stars seem to be so shy.

The speedy messenger keeps rushing,
I wish to hold it close,
The moon tells a different story,
Of the beauty of highs and lows.

The stairway to heaven beckons,
To climb every step,
All I wish is to be engulfed,
By the mysterious space on each step.

I See the lost ones,
Floating amongst the stars,
The beautiful skin of the night sky,
Has such beautiful scars.

I close my eyes and realise,
Even after all possible imaginations,
My thoughts are stars,
I can't fathom into constellations.

Simple As This

The feeling of content within,
The eternal happiness,
Could it be something as simple as this?

Tried to look through the questions,
But it only led me to where I should not go,
A shower of bullets from confusion guns.

Rolling down the window,
The cold wind straight on my face,
Inner peace knocked in the door.

The feeling of content within,
The eternal happiness,
Could it be something as simple as this?

Into the darkness far away,
Hung a tiny light bulb,
It's light guiding strangers astray.

The Mantra is to seek,
To seek what you want within,
To support the weak.

To live and let live
The magic is within all of us,
Could it be something as simple as this?

The Journey

You've grown so much,
I'm proud of you.

When you had started,
You had no hopes,
Still you made till today,
Grabbing the ropes.
You learnt to climb,
You learnt to get back up,
You learnt to cry and hide,
You learnt to not give up,
You aim for the sun,
You absorb the sunshine,
In the darkness of night,
You held on to the moonshine.
You have come a long way,
But still there's more,
So just carry on ahead,
And don't lose hope.

You Are Perfect

Let me look at you,
You are such a rare creation,
You are something special,
You have such a vision.

Strong like the rock at the bay,
Firm like the old tree,
Beautiful like the tiny flowers,
Happy like a bird set free.

You can be everything,
You Don't have to be told,
By everyone around you,
To open your mind manifold.

Just feel the fresh air,
Smile and imagine,
You standing at the Beach,
The sun setting and a mild wind.

Feel YOURSELF within you,
Explore yourself,
You will find the world within you,
The Best book in your shelf.

You are perfect who you are,
You deserve the Best of your love,
You Don't need to be someone else,
Because who you are is enough.

A Feeling

The smell of the rain,
Fresh on the ground,
Looking at the sky,
Listening to the sound.

She had been fighting,
The battles no one knew of,
Day in day out,
The time never seemed to stop.

He was a lonely kid,
Bullied every day for being weak,
He had planned to end it all,
To die by the end of the Week.

They sat together on the ground,
Without knowing what,
The other one was going through,
Or what were their thoughts.

Everyone fights some battles,
We are just at different levels,
Happiness is what everyone seeks,
But succumb to the devils.

They saved each other's lives,
Without knowing so,
They were so vibrant,
You could see their souls glow.

Get Back Up

Too much sadness,
Too many tears,
Hey there it's been a while,
So just get up and smile!

I know how much pain you feel,
Maybe I'll never feel the same,
But I'll try to understand,
And be a helping hand.

Do you feel like you are nothing?
Or no one possibly cares?
But hey! Things do get better,
Maybe sooner or later!

Everything happens,
The way it is supposed to happen,
All you have to do is keep going,
When they want you to cry, sing.

Prove everyone wrong,
You got this,
You can get through it,
However difficult it is.

So just smile there,
It won't solve your problems,
But it will give you the hope and strength,
To go on till the end.

Too much sadness,
Too many tears,
Hey there it's been a while,
So just get up and smile!

Perfection

A thing said is perfect,
If it is just felt.

Perfection is what we seek,
But who can define it?
Is it riches and wealth?
Or people who stay till your death?

Someone said it correctly,
Words can never capture it entirely,
Knowledge cannot be measured,
By the Grades secured.

Deep Inside us,
We all are made of the same particles,
The same ones that make the stars,
The moon and even the Mars.

We all are celestial,
Our thoughts being superficial,
But somewhere I think,
Our stars connect like rhythmic beats.

Our vibes Form an echo,
And it shines like Sun with Snow,
In a sky full of stars above the ocean so blue,
I think I saw you.

There is so much to learn from you,
Calmness, Humbleness, Being true,
I connect with you at a level,
So high above, it doesn't seem real.

You taught me a lot,
To be strong and to never stop,
I hope you don't See me,
As some boy caught up between dreams and reality.

Maybe we'll make mistakes,
But I feel that we will give what it takes,
To save the other from falling down,
And shout but never frown.

Do I even make sense?
Let's never get tense,
Laugh our way to the end,
Cry a little but then build bridges.

Climb mountains and cross streams,
Complete our dreams,
Find a way through forests with trees so high,
Let's just give it a try.

The stars beckon to shine,
Now, is the Best time of our life,
I will say this tomorrow too,
Because every day is new.

Our minds meet at a different level,
You are unique and special,
There can never be another you,
For whom I wrote something after thinking through.

I just hope,
The thread of the friendship becomes a rope,
When years later this day comes,
You and I will still be us.

Special

You have come a long way,
Too long to say,
How did it start and how did it reach here,
So let go of the fear,
The fear of being judged,
You have achieved very much.
Your journey is for you,
Not to make someone like you,
You are unique and so are your thoughts,
You are unique no matter what.
The journey will continue,
Fellow travellers will come too,
Some will stay,
Some will part the way,
But you stay strong,
One day someone will walk the road long.
That would be the best chapter,
Of your life and the journey will go farther.

Equality

Equality is what women seek,
I don't disagree with it.

Wanting to walk side by side,
with the men by their side.
Demanding the roles to be changed,
But isn't it a bit strange?
We came to this world,
With some role to play in this herd.
Women give birth to the children,
They are protected by the men.
This was the ancient rule,
Considering the ordeals women go through.
But hey! Ancient rules are stupid,
We can Deal with it!
I wonder if some day,
A Zebra gets up and hunts that day,
Kill a Lion and eat his meat,
"Oh I just wanted some equality!"
"All men are the same"
You feel you have a strong game,
But isn't that stereotyping?
It just gets me thinking.
When cosmetics are advertised heavily,
Why do you women take it dearly?

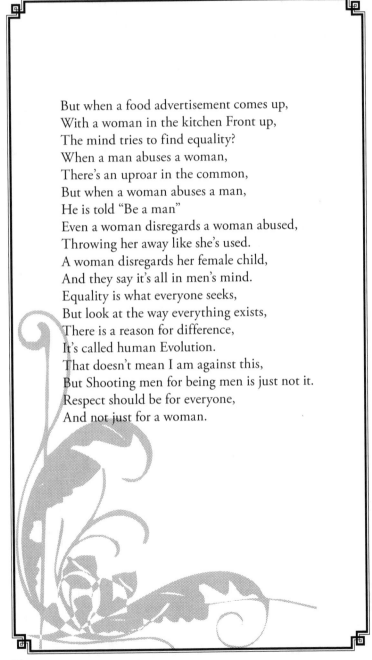

But when a food advertisement comes up,
With a woman in the kitchen Front up,
The mind tries to find equality?
When a man abuses a woman,
There's an uproar in the common,
But when a woman abuses a man,
He is told "Be a man"
Even a woman disregards a woman abused,
Throwing her away like she's used.
A woman disregards her female child,
And they say it's all in men's mind.
Equality is what everyone seeks,
But look at the way everything exists,
There is a reason for difference,
It's called human Evolution.
That doesn't mean I am against this,
But Shooting men for being men is just not it.
Respect should be for everyone,
And not just for a woman.

A Friend

What is a friend?
Going out partying? Or meeting daily?
No!
A friend is someone,
Who never lets you cry alone,
Who loves you for your every bone,
Who gives you sunglasses in the sun,
And holds an umbrella in the rain.
A friend is someone,
Who never lets you lose hope,
Who goes crazy if you feel low,
Who manages to put a smile,
Every time you got a tear in line.
A friend is someone,
Who touches you deep in your heart,
Who makes you feel like a piece of art,
You are that friend,
Years from now when I am nearing my end,
I'll look back and thank you,
For being so amazing and true,
We will have our crazy moments,
Both sad and happy,
But I'll never leave you till the end,
I'll never leave you till the end.

A Lost Soul

Why does the night seem so dark?
Ears long to listen to the melody,
In and around I search for a mark,
A sign or maybe even a hint,
A clue that might lead to you,
A quest I find myself in,
Frantically I search everything through,
But I could find nothing,
Then far away,
I see the familiar eyes,
A smile warmer than a bright summer day,
A sudden feeling of elation rushes,
Rushing through a flood of emotions,
I jump and try to run towards you,
Feet stay firm on the ground without any reason,
You put out your hand calling me towards you,
I apply all my might,
The Gods fear my strength,
But you start to move away from sight,
The smile inviting me towards you,
You slowly start moving away,
Slowly fading into the darkness,
Don't leave me! Don't go away,
You smile and wait,
"Look up" You say,
I See a Million stars,

"I'll always be with you, through night and day"
With the smile you fade away,
I scream, I shout,
I run to the place where you were,
But you are nowhere to be seen of found,
I look up and See your smile amongst the stars,
You are away,
But I keep thinking about you,
Every single day,
Your fading smile appears again,
Trying to meet you this time,
I wake up.

People don't leave us when they die.

Hope

H is for the Heights you have achieved,
O is for the Opportunities you have taken,
P is for the Pain you have endured,
E is for Everything you have been through
HOPE is not the future,
It's what you learn from your past,
So look at the bigger picture,
Try to let it go fast,
Learn from what has happened,
Keep hanging on to the rope,
Your present will be brightened,
You just need to keep up your hope.

A Soldier

I am your son mother,
In the low temperatures,
In the high altitudes,
In the dry deserts,
In the high seas,
And in the skies.

I am your son mother,
I try my best to remove the dirt,
I try to keep your home clean,
Even if I get hurt.

I am your son mother,
The chiefs earn their medals,
Even though it's me,
Who goes to the battle ground.

I am your son mother,
Who is considered a servant,
Even after I risk my life,
To safeguard your honor.

I am your son mother,
I may or may not go home again,
My wife still wait's for me,
My children wait to play with me in the rain.

I am your son mother,
I live my life for you,
I willingly die for you,
My love for you is so true.

I am your son mother,
I give everything,
So that my brothers and sisters sleep peacefully,
But I want to rest and hear my baby sing.

I am your son mother,
I long to see my children,
I crave to hear my wife,
I wait for the phone call from 9-10.

I am your son mother,
If I have to leave their side,
Promise me that you'll take care of them,
Tell them it will be a smooth ride.

I am your son mother,
Serving you is my only life goal,
Protecting your honour and your children,
To keep you one and whole.

I am your son mother,
In the low temperatures,
In the high altitudes,
In the dry deserts,
In the high seas,
And in the skies.

I am your son mother,
I am a soldier.

You Are Beautiful

The stars seem to shine upon you,
The moon tries to hide,
The flowers are jealous of you,
You are a beach on a high tide.
You are so beautiful!

You may not love yourself,
Or maybe even hate,
But just once see yourself,
Through my eyes' gate,
You are so beautiful!

The smile, the eyes,
The beautiful face and beautiful hair,
Reflecting the earth and the skies,
I could just forever stare,
You are so beautiful!

Don't let anyone tell you,
You aren't beautiful,
Because they don't see the real you,
And they just make themselves a fool,
You are so beautiful!

No weight is over,
No face is prettier,
No one's beauty is higher or lower,
Everyone is beautiful and unique here,
You are so beautiful!

Just keep smiling always,
Don't lose that smile,
Because that's what completes your face,
That's who you are and that's your style,
You are so beautiful!

This Time Shall Pass

Your life seems so complicated,
You don't see any way out of it,
Everything's spinning in your head,
It seems like an endless pit.
But don't you give up,
This bad time shall pass,
Just breathe and look up,
And absorb the strength from the stars.
You will keep fighting,
However long it takes,
You will learn to sing,
In the world so fake.
You feel you are changed,
You aren't the person you were,
The old you is dead,
Because people change only for the better.
The sun will shine again,
In the sea of your life,
To remove all your pain,
Choose a flower and not a knife.
I am not a fortune teller,
I can't predict the future,
But I'm sure it's better,
Because you are stronger than you were.
You can do it,
I believe in you,
You can make through it,
I believe in you.

Missing Someone

Like the waves on the beach,
Like the wind that tries to reach,
I miss you.

The cold wind that blew,
The early morning dew,
The food that saw us through,
I miss that too.

The sun shone so brightly,
Someone did say it rightly,
We have held on to it tightly,
I miss it truly.

We ran, we cycled, we played,
Wish we could have forever stayed,
It's like for each other we are made,
I miss the memories which never fade.

The smiles, the tears,
The conquering of fears,
Nowhere else on the 8 spheres,
I miss the peers.

Like the waves on the beach,
Like the wind that tries to reach,
I miss you.

Box It Out

When you're down,
And they want to climb the hell out of you,
I want to show you how to,
Use doubter's fuel,
Convert it to gunpowder too.
Now just blow the candles off,
Engulf yourself into the darkness,
Think about what makes you strong,
Build up the energy,
Feel like you don't have any worries,
Think of your problems,
Look into their eyes,
Jab, jab, hook.
Thrash the hell out of it,
Don't let it get it to you,
Get your damn hands up,
Defend your face from the blows,
Dodge a punch and land a cross,
When it is vulnerable,
Just knock it off with an uppercut.
See? You won!
That's how you fight!
Hold someone as your reason to fight,
Ask someone to be your guide,
I know you will win,
It maybe tough but you will!

Hope In Your Heart

We're going to be alright,
So wipe your tears and hold tight,
I've got news for you,
The sun is shining and so are you.

You are going to light up the world,
You have my word,
This life is going to lift you up,
Fill your happiness cup.

You have walls around your heart,
But all I see is your beautiful stars,
I won't let you go,
Hold my hand and carry on.

We've seen darkness and the light,
But your light is so bright,
It shows me light in darkness,
You deserve the best and nothing less.

It's not too late,
I see hope in your heart,
Sometimes you lose,
Sometimes you shoot broken arrows in the dark,.

You seek a person,
Someone who is for you,
Tear down the walls of your heart,
Take my hand I'll be with you!

The world is beautiful,
So get up and break the rule,
Let's live our life and be happy,
Hold my hand fly away!

Be Brave

It's just one of those days,
When you can't even feel your face,
You get lost in so many ways,
Caught up in life's race.

You pretend to be happy,
Trying to fit in,
But inside you feel so heavy,
You feel like a blank person with skin.

What are we achieving?
Out of this races we race?
We suffer the same as a king!
What is success without a happy face?

We have lost our feelings,
In order to get paper,
We got our body up and running,
But our mind continues to hover.

What are we making of these lives?
Do we serve any purpose?
Do we actually exist?
Or are we fragments of a dream of a person?

In our quest to win,
We forget to enjoy the road,
In order to win the swim,
We forgot the fishes and the poor toad.

Climbing the tree is more important,
Than enjoying the flowers beneath,
We have become so hesitant,
We even smile without showing our teeth!

So afraid of being judged,
Trying to be perfect for the world,
Enjoying your thoughts is overpowered,
By the quest of being heard.

The sooner we realise,
The better our lives will be,
Shine and rise among hatred and despise,
Even a desert can grow a tree.

Do what makes you smile,
Do what you won't regret for not doing,
Let your passion be your style,
Let your confidence be a sting.

Where you succeed in conquering patience,
There lies your success,
Go out and enjoy the dance,
Don't cry but enjoy the little mess.

Ask yourself if you are happy,
With the daily torture you suffer,
No your life isn't crappy,
If you make yourself tougher.

Enjoy every single minute today,
Rather than crying about it later,
Celebrate every night and day,
Just live your life and make it better!

Be Proud Of Who You Are

You stand in the crowd,
You feel like you are an outcast,
A reject and someone left on the ground.

You try to fit in,
Try to blend yourself into everyone,
Try to absorb yourself in their skin.

But you don't blend into everyone,
You try to be like a person,
Who is liked and adored by everyone.

But you don't realise,
The person never tried to be someone,
The pretence dies.

You feel low,
You don't know how to cope up,
Your goal is about to blow!

That's what goes wrong,
Never try to be someone,
Have a belief very strong.

You may be a bit healthy,
A bit introvert,
Or a bit silly.

You may be nervous,
Anxious, obnoxious or not "cool"
Maybe you are not famous like others.

But that doesn't say,
You are not the best,
It says that there will be one day.

When people will love you,
For the way you are,
For your soul so true.

If you feel you are fat,
Or if you are so different,
Lay those thoughts down flat.

If you feel ugly,
You won't be loved,
Just look into a mirror quickly.

You need to realise,
That not every flower is the same,
Whether there's rain or sunshine.

Don't be reluctant,
You will be judged and called names,
Feel yourself being elegant.

They will try to pull you down,
No matter what you do,
Because they know, you deserve that crown.

Let your mind just steer,
Towards what you want to do,
Let you guts conquer the fear.

If you ever doubt your ability,
Just because someone says that you cannot,
Their thoughts don't have a validity.

A wallflower wouldn't exist,
If there was no will and self believe,
To be a shining light in the mist.

Bullies can go haywire,
Never let them demoralise,
Use them as a tire.

The tire of your success car,
Fuel can be the hatred,
See yourself go away so far!

I know it must be difficult,
To love yourself when all you got was hate,
Whether you are a child or an adult.

People keep hating you,
They keep on judging,
whether you are false or true.

Be awesome!
Be proud of yourself!
Leave them awestruck!

A Letter To Humanity

Dear Humanity,

In the middle of night,
In the absence of sight,
I searched for you.

Looked through the flowers,
With my uncanny powers,
You were nowhere to be found.

Through every grain of sand,
On every piece of land,
You were nowhere to be found.

I looked through the butterflies,
The seas and the skies,
You were nowhere to be found.

In the people with suits and ties,
Who can even stop the time that flies,
You were nowhere to be found.

In the super cars,
In the dust that blew blocking the stars,
You were nowhere to be found.

In the dead sea fish,
Consumed by the oily dish,
You were nowhere to be found.

Through our mother's age of teen,
Through her transition to brown from green,
You were nowhere to be found.

In the times of need,
Surrounded by greed,
You were nowhere to be found.

Even in the 7 billion opportunities,
Across the villages and the cities,
You were nowhere found.

When rivers of blood replaced rivers of water,
When the lives became hotter,
You were nowhere to be found.

Amidst the tears of the children,
And the suffering of the women,
You were nowhere to be found.

When there was no sight,
When they were in plight,
You were nowhere to be found.

When a mother cried,
For her baby who died,
You were nowhere to be found.

In the "fun" of teasing,
The wrath of bullying,
You were nowhere to be found.

Innocence decided to try,
But even it couldn't help but cry,
Still, you were nowhere to be found.

When the ones with green paper,
Were considered better,
You were nowhere to be found.

In the ice cold weather,
To destroy they gather,
You were nowhere to be found.

When a baby slept hungry,
And someone went on food wasting spree,
You were nowhere to be found.

I just hope you come out of hiding,
Escape the rules abiding,
Because I don't want the future,
To start another search.

Don't say I didn't try.
In the middle of the night,
In the absence of sight,
I searched for you.

Death

I've waited long to see what you are,
Are you a person?
Are you just a phase?
These questions have made me wonder,
What it's like to embrace you?

You are an old friend,
A sister of my mother life,
So aunt death will you tell me?
What it's like to embrace you?

I long now to see what you behold,
Even being so mysterious,
You make us talk about you,
What it's like to embrace you?

The entire life,
I've lived fearing you,
Thinking how you would be,
What it's like to embrace you?

Now as I approach you,
Will you take me to my friends?
Are they with you? And do they know?
What it's like to embrace you?

What magic do you have?
I've wondered about you my whole life,
And now I'm afraid to face you,
What it's like to embrace you?

A Treasure

It's an ocean,
I'm drowning in,
I want to get out,
But I want to stay in.

In the middle of the Dead,
The ones buried beneath,
So much treasure lies hidden,
No, not of Gold or money,
A treasure of thoughts,
Ideas that never made it,
The unsaid things,
The would have beens,
The ifs and buts,
The Situations which never happened,
The memories which will never happen,
The treasure that will never be understood,
It's the treasure growing day by day.

Life Is A Journey And Not A Race

Life is a journey and not a race,
It is the truth we don't want to face.

There are moments,
Where things Don't go as planned,
When everything goes against,
You feel tired and exhausted.
Remember this is just a Phase,
You will see better days,

Things keep happening,
People keep coming and going,
Hold on to the ones who show,
That they would stay during sun and snow.
Maybe you feel no one understands,
But there are people who will try,
Someone would be there to know,
That your darkness cannot replace your glow,
Let them know you care too,
Sometimes you don't know what hides beneath,
What hides under the smile,
It's dark at times,
But it's a bright smile outside.
Make people happy,
It's a race everyone is running,
A race which has no finish line,
So by the time the fuel ends,
It's too late to refuel and start again.
The water flows and it rains,
Happiness resides where pain ends.

Make the days better,
But just remember,
No matter what levels of success you reach,
Remember the people who Help you get there.

Life is a journey and not a race,
It's a truth we don't want to face

Oblivion

Lift off the blindfold,
I see again.

Reaching out to the stars,
I jumped across,
Floating in the night sky,
Wondering what happens after we die,
Expecting my mind to flow,
Through the days waiting for it to grow,
Just across, I see the moon,
Floating on the ship of my thoughts,
I wander towards it,
The world stops spinning,
Everything disappears,
All around me is a black dense void,
Closing my eyes,
The music plays faster,
I float aimlessly through the void,
The stars start twinkling,
The earth spins majestically,
What is there beyond where my eyes can see?
Is there anything which my mind can't percieve?
The stars seem to lay down a path of light,
The oblivion await's,
Beyond the wildest thoughts,
The void engulfed my soul,
I feel free, I dance,
Dancing to the rhythm of nothing,

The music stops for a while,
As I look around me,
I feel something Inside me,
A Desire to look for something which doesn't exist,
To fly across the void,
To go beyond imagination,
The world await's the knowledge beyond existence,
I feel peace seeping in,
The eternal Revelation of purity,
A Vision in disguise,
Not to be intelligent, but to be wise.

The oblivion will strike,
The days will end, the mighty will Fall,
I'll be ready then,
For now, I just want to dream.

-SHREY.

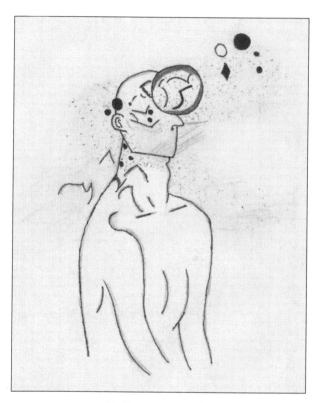

By Emma Fousek.

Printed in the United States
By Bookmasters